MW00379712

CC960: JOURNEY TOWARD WHOLENESS

REV. DON CROSSLAND

Textbook for the Course:
Refocusing Your Passions
by Rev. Don Crossland

05/03/04

Christian Life Educators Network (CLEN) is a world-wide network of member schools in affiliation with CLST Global. CLEN offers complete support services to member schools and students. Through an articulation agreement with CLST Global, students in CLEN schools can earn CLST Global Certificates, Diplomas and Degrees.

Christian Life School of Theology Global (CLST Global) has met the requirements for exemption from applicable Georgia law as a religious institution under the provision of the Post-secondary Educational Authorization Act, Georgia Code 20-3-100 et seq. As a result, CLST Global awards a variety of Ministry Certificates, Diplomas and Degrees ranging from an Associate of Theology through a Doctor of Sacred Studies.

©Christian Life School of Theology Global, Inc.

Table of Contents

Chapter 1

Introduction

This course provides a spiritual and emotional growth model with a Biblical perspective. The emphasis of this model is the process of restoration. Ultimately, it is through a growing relationship with Jesus Christ and others that one experiences wholeness. By removing barriers to these relationships, believers may come to know Him intimately—the One who meets our deepest needs and longings; the only true God and our Savior Jesus Christ. This in turn will better equip us to fulfill our destiny in the body of Christ.

Restoration Defined

Three different Greek words are used in the New Testament for restoration. They are:

1. αποδιδομι *(apodidomi)*—To give back that which was lost

   And Zacchaeus stopped and said to the Lord, "Behold, Lord, half of my possessions I will give to the poor, and if I have defrauded anyone of anything, I will give back four times as much." (Luke 19:8)

2. αποκατηρστημι *(apokathestimi)*—To restore to a former condition of well being (health, finances, spiritual)

   And it came about on another Sabbath, that He entered the synagogue and was teaching; and there was a man there whose right hand was withered. And the scribes and the Pharisees were watching Him closely, to see if He healed on the Sabbath, in order that they might find reason to accuse Him. But He knew what they were thinking, and He said to the man with the withered hand, "Arise and come forward!" And he rose and came forward. And Jesus said to them, "I ask you, is it lawful on the Sabbath to do good, or to do evil, to save life or to destroy it?" And after looking around at them all, He said to him, "Stretch out your hand!" And he did so; and his hand was completely restored. (Luke 6:6-10)

3. καταρτιζο *(katartizo)*—To mend, or furnish completely, to fix or complete

Brethren, If a man is caught in any trespass, you who are spiritual, restore such a one in a spirit of gentleness; each one looking to yourself, lest you too be tempted. Bear one another's burdens, and thus fulfill the law of Christ. (Galatians 6:1-2)

The word "caught" (προλαμβανο—*rolambano*) in *Galatians 6:1* means overtaken beforehand. When one is overtaken by any trespass, we are to "restore such a one" in gentleness. However, restoration means more than restraining from harmful and sinful behavior. It involves mending past hurts, completing unfulfilled needs, and restoring the soul for Kingdom purposes. It is not just behavior modification. It is the process (active, continuous action) of change in the inner core of our being. Restoration may involve events in our lives that impact our spiritual growth; it is a process of growth and maturity.

The Process of Restoration

As we understand the biblical meaning of restoration, we must also consider the process of restoring one to wholeness. What are some of the elements involved in the restoration process?

A. CONSIDERING THE PAST

As mentioned above, restoration involves mending past hurts, completing unfulfilled needs and restoring the soul for Kingdom purposes. Addressing the unresolved issues of our past can be a key to the restoration process.

1. GAIN INSIGHT INTO YOUR PAST

Answering the objections...

...the old things passed away, behold, new things have come. (2 Corinthians 5:17)

...forgetting what lies behind and reaching forward to what lies ahead. (Philippians 3:13)

...lay aside the old self. (Ephesians 4:22)

...forgiving each other. (Ephesians 4:32)

2. DETERMINE HOW YOUR HISTORY IS AFFECTING YOU TODAY.

Delving into the past and staying there is not healthy. But, the Holy Spirit, who convicts us of our sins, can give us insight about how our past is affecting the present. A key to healing and restoration is spiritual perception: *"For the mind set on the flesh is death, but the mind set on the Spirit is life and peace,"* (Romans 8:6). The Holy Spirit can show us how we are acting out the hurts or unfulfilled needs of the past. He can help us see and then release the lies we have accepted as reality. The Spirit can also help free us from the sinful systems of behavior that were our means of coping or surviving.

3. ALLOW GOD TO TURN PAST HURTS INTO PRESENT VICTORY.

With new insight about ourselves and with the guidance of the Holy Spirit, we can let God work His gracious miracle and turn the hurts of the past into victories for today. He does that for His people: *"God causes all things to work together for good to those who love God."* (Romans 8:28) This is a promise we can claim as we surrender our hurts, our failures and our wills to our heavenly Father.

B. THE ROLE OF THE CHURCH

The church's part in the process is to provide the following three expressions of ministry:

1. THE CHURCH IS TO BE A SPIRITUAL HOSPITAL FOR THE WOUNDED.

The Spirit of the Lord is upon Me, because He anointed Me to preach the gospel to the poor. He has sent Me to proclaim release to the captives, and recovery of sight to the blind, to set free those who are downtrodden, to proclaim the favorable year of the Lord. (Luke 4:18-19)

2. THE CHURCH IS TO BE A TRAINING SCHOOL FOR DISCIPLES.

Go therefore and make disciples of all nations, baptizing them in the name of the Father and the Son and the Holy Spirit, teaching them to observe all that I commanded you; and lo, I am with you always, even to the end of the age. (Matthew 28: 19-20)

3. THE CHURCH IS TO BE AN ARMY FOR OVERCOMING THE ENEMY AND POSSESSING THE LAND.

Finally, be strong in the Lord, and in the strength of His might. Put on the full armor of God, that you may be able to stand firm against the schemes of the devil. For our struggle is not against flesh and blood, but against the rulers, against the powers, against the world forces of this darkness, against the spiritual forces of wickedness in the heavenly places. Therefore, take up the full armor of God, that you

may be able to resist in the evil day, and having done everything, to stand firm. Stand firm therefore, having girded your loins with truth, and having put on the breastplate of righteousness, and having shod your feet with the preparation of the gospel of peace; in addition to all, taking up the shield of faith with which you will be able to extinguish all the flaming missiles of the evil one. And take the helmet of salvation and the sword of the Spirit, which is the word of God. With all prayer and petition pray at all times in the Spirit, and with this in view, be on the alert with all perseverance and petition for all the saints. (Ephesians 6: 10-18)

The Stages of Restoration

The following sections identify the wounds of our past, evaluate how they effect us presently and how they can be healed and replaced with healthy behavior.

INSIGHTS INTO OUR HISTORY	PRESENT RESULTS	RESTORATION PROCESS
Childhood wounds and resulting losses *John 10:10*	Resulting consequences of wrong responses to loss *Romans 1:18-32, 2 Corinthians 7:10*	Transformation through regeneration and renewal *Titus 3:1-7, Acts 2:41-47*
Lack of moral teaching and standards	Faulty belief system	**REFRAMING** Replacing false belief systems with truth
Lack of nurturing and emotional closeness	Unmet spiritual, emotional and physical needs	**REBONDING** Replacing wrong relationships with healthy relationships
Lack of wisdom and perception	Inadequate and immature responses to difficult life circumstances	**REANCHORING** Replacing immature human response with God's wisdom
Lack of convictions and limitations	Improper boundaries and convictions	**REBUILDING** Replacing human standards and boundaries with God's standards
Lack of vision and purpose	Faulty value system	**REDIRECTING** Replacing lack of purpose and joy with a new vision and enthusiasm

Chapter 2

Releasing Shame

But we have renounced the things hidden because of shame, not walking in craftiness or adulterating the word of God, but by manifestation of truth commending ourselves to every man's conscience in the sight of God. (2 Corinthians 4:2)

W hat is shame? Webster defines shame as a "painful emotion caused by consciousness of guilt, shortcoming or impropriety." There is a distinct difference between guilt and shame: Guilt is the result of violating our conscience—doing something through our words, thoughts, and actions which violates our values and beliefs. It comes from doing something we believe to be wrong. Shame is the result of not meeting the expectations or approval of others, or by being looked down upon by others. A key to understanding shame is recognizing that there are two types.

The Causes and Expressions of Shame

A. TWO TYPES OF SHAME

Healthy Shame—"I made a mistake." (Adam and Eve)

This type of shame enables us to say, "I made a mistake," "I sinned," and "I am responsible for my actions." We experience a healthy sense of shame when we realize we have done something wrong. Experiences that bring on these reactions remind us of our limitations as human beings in need of a Savior.

Unhealthy Shame—"I am a mistake." (Moses)

When we feel an unhealthy sense of shame we have thoughts like, "I am a mistake," and I'm flawed and unworthy." Healthy shame comes because of something we've done, but unhealthy shame results because of something done to us. People feeling unhealthy shame regret who they are. They regret their being rather than their behavior.

B. CAUSES OF UNHEALTHY SHAME

The causes of unhealthy shame are many and varied. It can result at any point in life—from as early as the womb, through traumatic childhood experiences and on into adulthood. Unhealthy shame results when we receive as truth a lie about ourselves and our worth. This can be experienced at a very personal level as well as passed down through family generations. Below are listings of some common causes and characteristics of unhealthy shame:

1. PERSONAL SHAME:

⟨ Words, phrases, statements, nick names, putdowns and jokes

⟨ Abuse—physical, emotional and sexual

⟨ Rejection and abandonment

⟨ Unmet spiritual, emotional and physical needs

⟨ Mistakes and failures

⟨ Comparing ourselves with society's standards

⟨ Unrealistic expectations

2. FAMILY SHAME:

Family shame can be the result of not living up to the expectations and rules of society. When the approval of man is more valued than the approval of God, the family rules become rooted in the desire to avoid shame—even healthy shame. Thus, family discipline is not based on correcting to change, but punishing to stop behavior that can bring shame. This level of unhealthy shame is often passed down to future generations.

Causes of Family Shame

〈 Scandal • Financial Failure • Racial and Ethnic Background

Characteristics of Family Shame		Elements of Godly Relating
Man's approval	vs.	God's approval
Outward image	vs.	Inward character
Secrecy	vs.	Openness
Chaos	vs.	Calm
Inappropriate Roles	vs.	Gifts
Isolation	vs.	Closeness
Denial	vs.	Awareness
Blaming others	vs.	Personal Responsibilities
Lack of closure	vs.	Resolutions
Triangular communications	vs.	Direct Communications

Cycles of Shame

C. RESULTS OF UNHEALTHY SHAME

〈 Produces a false identity

〈 Reenacts itself

〈 Inability to accept compliments

〈 Lacks boundaries

〈 Spirals

〈 Develops into addictive behavior

〈 Shames others

〈 Causes passivity

〈 Chooses death

Releasing Personal Shame

1. **REPENT OF OUR UNBELIEF;** repent from continuing to carry the unhealthy shame and for not living in the provisions that are in Christ

   For this reason we must pay much closer attention to what we have heard, lest we drift away from it. For if the word spoken through angels proved unalterable, and every transgression and disobedience received a just recompense, how shall we escape if we neglect so great a salvation? (Hebrews 2:1-3a)

2. **CHOOSE NOT TO AGREE WITH SATAN;** he is "the accuser of the brethren." Instead, accept God's grace and covering through Jesus Christ who bore our shame.

   Since then the children share in flesh and blood, He Himself likewise also partook of the same, that through death He might render powerless him who had the power of death, that is, the devil; and might deliver those who through fear of death were subject to slavery all their lives. (Hebrews 2:14-15)

3. **GIVE THE RESPONSIBILITY BACK** to the person through whom the shame came and fully forgive and release them from bitter judgments.

(Matthew 18:1-35)

4. **RECLAIM THE BLESSINGS AND PURPOSES OF GOD** for your life, which were interrupted and sabotaged by Satan.

Having therefore such a hope, we use great boldness in our speech, and are not as Moses, who used to put a veil over his face that the sons of Israel might not look intently at the end of what was fading away. But their minds were hardened; for until this very day at the reading of the old covenant the same veil remains unlifted, because it is removed in Christ. But to this day whenever Moses is read, a veil lies over their heart; but whenever a man turns to the Lord, the veil is taken away. Now the Lord is the Spirit; and where the Spirit of the Lord is, there is liberty. But we all, with unveiled face beholding as in a mirror the glory of the Lord, are being transformed into the same image from glory to glory, just as from the Lord, the Spirit. (2 Corinthians 3:12-18)

5. **BEGIN TO EXPRESS GRATITUDE TO GOD** for how He is going to turn the unhealthy shame into transparency and joy for His glory and for your benefit.

Therefore, since we receive a kingdom which cannot be shaken, let us show gratitude, by which we may offer to God an acceptable service with reverence and awe; for our God is a consuming fire. (Hebrews 12:29)

6. **STIR UP THE GIFT OF GOD WITHIN YOU** by calling to memory His blessings on and through you.

And for this reason I remind you to kindle afresh the gift of God which is in you through the laying on of hands. For God has not given us a spirit of timidity, but of power and love and discipline. Therefore do not be ashamed of the testimony of our Lord, or of me His prisoner; but join with me in suffering for the gospel according to the power of God, who has saved us, and called us with a holy calling, not according to our works, but according to His own purpose and grace which was granted us in Christ Jesus from all eternity, but now has been revealed by the appearing of our Savior Christ Jesus, who abolished death, and brought life and immortality to light through the gospel, for which I was appointed a preacher and an apostle and a teacher. For this reason I also suffer these things, but I am not ashamed; for I know whom I have believed and I am convinced that He is able to guard what I have entrusted to Him until that day. Retain the standard of sound words which you have heard from me, in the faith and love which are in Christ Jesus. Guard, through the Holy Spirit who dwells in us, the treasure which has been entrusted to you. (2 Timothy 1:6-14)

7. **BECOME A PART OF AN EXTENDED FAMILY** (local church) which can mirror back to you God's love and grace.

Let us hold fast the confession of our hope without wavering, for He who promised is faithful; and let us consider how to stimulate one another to love and good deeds, not forsaking our own assembling together, as is the habit of some, but encourage one another; and all the more, as you see the day drawing near. (Hebrews 10:23-25)

Dealing with Family Shame

1. ACKNOWLEDGE IT

So I gave my attention to the Lord God to seek Him by prayer and supplications, with fasting, sackcloth, and ashes. And I prayed to the Lord my God and confessed and said, "Alas, O Lord, the great and awesome God, who keeps His covenant and lovingkindness for those who love Him and keep His commandments, we have sinned, committed iniquity, acted wickedly, and rebelled, even turning aside from Thy commandments and ordinances. Moreover, we have not listened to Thy servants the prophets, who spoke in Thy name to our kings, our princes, our fathers, and all the people of the land. Righteousness belongs to Thee, O Lord, but to us open up Judah, the inhabitants of Jerusalem, and all Israel, those who are near by and those who are far away in all the countries to which Thou hast driven them, because of their unfaithful deeds which they have committed against Thee. Open shame belongs to us, O Lord, to our kings, our princes, and our fathers, because we have sinned against Thee. To the Lord our God belong compassion and forgiveness, for we have rebelled against Him; nor have we obeyed the voice of the Lord our God, to walk in His teachings which He set before us through His servants the prophets. Indeed all Israel has transgressed Thy law and turned aside, not obeying Thy voice; so the curse has been poured out on us, along with the oath which is written in the law of Moses the servant of God, for we have sinned against Him. Thus He has confirmed His words which He had spoken against us, and against our rulers who ruled us, to bring on us great calamity; for under the whole heaven there has not been done anything like what was done to Jerusalem. As it is written in the Law of Moses, all this calamity has come on us; yet we have not sought the favor of the Lord our God by turning from our iniquity and giving attention to Thy truth. Therefore, the Lord has kept the calamity in store and brought it on us; for the Lord our God is righteous with respect to all His deeds which He has done, but we have not obeyed His voice. And now, O Lord our God, who hast brought Thy people out of the land of Egypt with a mighty hand and hast made a name for Thyself, as it is this day—we have sinned, we have been wicked. O Lord, in accordance with all Thy righteous acts, let now Thine anger and Thy wrath turn away from Thy city Jerusalem, Thy holy mountain; for because of our sins and the iniquities of our fathers, Jerusalem and Thy people have become a reproach to all those around us. So now, our God, listen to the prayer of Thy servant and to his supplications, and for Thy sake, O Lord, let Thy face shine on Thy desolate sanctuary. O my God, incline Thine ear and hear! Open Thine eyes and see our desolations and the city which is called by Thy name; for we are not presenting our supplications before Thee on account of any merits of our own, but on account of Thy great compassion. O Lord, hear! O Lord, forgive! O Lord, listen and take action! For Thine own sake, O my God, do not delay, because Thy city and Thy people are called by Thy name. (Daniel 9:3-19)

2. SHARE IT WITH APPROPRIATE PERSONS

Therefore, confess our sins to one another, and pray for one another, so that you may be healed. The effective prayer of a righteous man can accomplish much. (James 5:17)

3. REPOSITION ROLE IN FAMILY

And do not be conformed to this world, but be transformed by the renewing of your mind, that you may prove what the will of God is, that which is good and acceptable and perfect. (Romans 12:2)

4. BE PREPARED FOR FAMILY CONFLICTS

Do not think that I came to bring peace on the earth; I did not come to bring peace, but a sword. For I cam to set a man against his father, and a daughter against her mother, and a daughter-in-law against her mother-in-law; and a man's enemies will be the members of his household. He who loves father or mother more than Me is not worthy of Me; and he who loves son or daughter more than Me is not worthy of Me. And he who does not take his cross and follow after Me is not worthy of Me. He who has found his life shall lose it, and he who has lost his life for My sake shall find it. (Matthew 10:34-39)

5. COMMUNICATE DIRECTLY WITH PERSON(S) INVOLVED

And if your brother sins, go and reprove him in private; if he listens to you, you have won your brother. But if he does not listen to you, take one or two more with you, so that by the mouth of two or three witnesses every fact my be confirmed. (Matthew 18:15-16)

6. RESPOND TO OFFENSES WITH GRACE AND FORGIVENESS

And be kind to one another, tender-hearted, forgiving each other, just as God in Christ also has forgiven you. (Ephesians 4:32)

7. MAINTAIN SELF-IDENTITY IN CHRIST, not in family system.

Therefore, since we have so great a cloud of witnesses surrounding us, let us also lay aside every encumbrance, and the sin which so easily entangles us, and let us run with endurance the race that is set before us, fixing our eyes on Jesus, the author and perfecter of faith, who for the joy set before Him endured the cross, despising the shame, and has sat down at the right hand of the throne of God. (Hebrews 12:1-2)

Chapter 3

Reframing–Part I

Identifying Faulty Belief Systems

A faulty belief system is a lifestyle resulting from wrong thoughts and actions learned and developed in an attempt to meet our personal needs or to avoid being hurt. It is viewing life through natural senses and not through God's perspective. (Romans 1:25).

A Faulty Belief System

A. A SYSTEM OF LIES ABOUT GOD

Behind every false belief system is a series of lies that we believe about God and His character.

> *Now the serpent was more crafty than any beast of the field which the Lord God had made. And he said to the woman, "Indeed, has God said, 'You shall not eat from any tree of the garden'?"*
> *And the woman said to the serpent, "From the fruit of the trees of the garden we may eat; but from the fruit of the tree which is in the middle of the garden, God has said, 'You shall not eat from it or touch it, lest you die'."*
> *And the serpent said to the woman, "You shall not die! For God knows that in the day you eat from it your eyes will be opened, and you will be like God, knowing good and evil." (Genesis 3:1-5)*

1. LIE NUMBER ONE:

"You shall not eat from any tree of the Garden . . ."(Genesis 3:1)

God is not able or will not meet our basic needs:

⟨   God didn't

⟨   Maybe God won't

⟨   Maybe God can't

⟨   Maybe God isn't

Lie against God the Father

Every good thing bestowed and every perfect gift is from above, coming down from the Father of lights, with whom there is no variation, or shifting shadow. (James 1:17)

2. LIE NUMBER TWO:

"You shall not surely die . . ."(Genesis 3:4)

There are no consequences resulting from our choices which violate God's word and our conviction.

Lie against Jesus Christ

For the wages of sin is death, but the free gift of God is eternal life in Christ Jesus our Lord. (Romans 6:23)

3. LIE NUMBER THREE:

"You will be like God . . ."(Genesis 3:5)

If our basic needs are going to be met, we will have to meet them ourselves, especially since we have not been able to trust God or our parents.

Lie against the Holy Spirit

Now to Him who is able to do exceeding abundantly beyond all that we ask or think, according to the power that works within us . . . (Ephesians 3:20)

Dismantling the Schemes

Understanding the Schemes and Strategies of Satan *Genesis 2:3-9, 15-17; 3:1-7; Ephesians 5:10-18*	Dismantling the Schemes and Strategies of Satan *2 Corinthians 10:3-5*
1. The strategy of speculations: *"Has God said?"* ← Leaves out part of the Word *"You shall not eat from any tree of the garden."* ← Adds to the Word *"You shall not eat from it or touch it"* ← Changes the Word *"Lest you die"*	1. Destroying speculations *"We are destroying speculations…" (2 Corinthians 10:5)*
1. The strategy of lies: ← God cannot or will not meet your basic needs. *"You shall not eat from any tree of the garden."* ← There are no consequences from our choices which violate God's word. *"You shall not surely die"* ← If our basic needs are going to be met, we will have to meet them ourselves, since we have not been able to trust God or our parents. *"You shall be as gods"*	2. Destroying lies against the knowledge of God *"…and every lofty thing raised up against the knowledge of God…" (2 Corinthians 10:5)*
1. The strategy of diversion ← Lust of the flesh *"The woman saw that the tree was good for food."* ← The lust of the eyes *"It was a delight to the eyes"* ← Pride of life *"Desirable to make one wise"*	3. Taking every thought captive to the obedience of Christ *"…and we are taking every thought captive to the obedience of Christ." (2 Corinthians 10:5)*

Continuing to stand against the lies of the enemy involves putting on the whole armor of God (Ephesians 6:10-20)

B. A SYSTEM OF LIES ABOUT OURSELVES

Not only does a person's beliefs about God get distorted, but an understanding of his own identity in Christ also gets distorted and faulty.

> *They exchanged the truth of God for a lie... (Romans 1:25a)*

"No one would love me if they really knew me. I can't measure up to people's expectations, especially God's."

> *But God demonstrated His love toward us, in that while we were yet sinners, Christ died for us (Romans 5:8)*

"I am unworthy and undeserving. This is caused by a wrong self image and low self esteem."

> *Blessed be the God and Father of our Lord Jesus Christ, who has blessed us with every spiritual blessing the heavenly places in Christ (Ephesians 1:3).*

"I can't trust others to meet my needs and they will never be met if I don't meet them. I've asked God, and nothing happened."

> *My God shall supply all your needs according to His riches in glory in Christ Jesus (Philippians 4:19).*

C. A SYSTEM OF LIES ABOUT OTHERS

"You can't trust others"

"Use others before they use you"

D. A SYSTEM OF LIES ABOUT LIFE

"Life isn't fair therefore, I can't be fair either if I'm to make it."

> *And we know that God causes all things to work together for good to those who love God, to those who are called according to His purpose.. (Romans 8:28)*

Mortality vs. Immortality

> *And He told them a parable, saying, "The land of a certain rich man was very productive." And he began reasoning to himself, saying, 'What shall I do, since I*

have no place to store my crops?' " And he said, 'This is what I will do: I will tear down my barns and build larger ones, and there I will store all my grain and my goods. And I will say to my soul, "Soul, you have many goods laid up for many years to come; take your ease, eat, drink and be merry.'" But God said to him, "You fool! This very night your soul is required of you; and now who will own what you have prepared?" So is the man who lays up treasure for himself, and is not rich toward God. (Luke 12:16-21)

E. A SYSTEM OF LIES ABOUT PAST FAILURE

"I am the sum of my past."

"Since I made a mistake, I am a mistake."

> *Therefore if any man is in Christ, he is a new creature; the old things passed away; behold, new things have come. (2 Corinthians 5:17)*

F. A SYSTEM OF LIES ABOUT HAPPINESS

"Peace, happiness and joy are based on circumstances."

> *Peace I leave with you; My peace I give to you; not as the world gives, do I give to you. Let now your heart be troubled, not let it be fearful. (John 14:27)*

Consequences of Faulty Belief Systems

Once a faulty belief system has been established, our values and actions will follow accordingly. It is foolish to go against God's truth and to reject His way. In scripture we are warned,

> *There is a way which seems right unto man, but its end is as the way of death. (Proverbs 16:25)*

One reason for our rejection and bitterness against God is because we have compared ourselves with others and judged that we have been short-changed in life. This results in jealousy and envy of others. Thus in our natural reasoning we conclude that if we are ever going to get what we deserve and have a right to, we must do it ourselves in our way. This results in selfish ambition. This kind of ambition has a disregard for the success and benefit of God's Kingdom and for others. The epistle of James clearly describes this condition:

> *Who among you is wise and understanding? Let him show by his good behavior his deeds in the gentleness of wisdom. But if you have bitter jealousy and selfish ambition in your heart, do not be arrogant and so lie against the truth. This wisdom is not that which comes down from above, but is earthly, natural, demonic.*

For where jealousy and selfish ambition exist, there is disorder and every evil thing. But the wisdom from above is first pure, then peaceable, gentle, reasonable, full of mercy and good fruit, unwavering, without hypocrisy. And the seed whose fruit is righteousness is sown in peace by those who make peace. (James 3:13-18)

Earthly —Our view of time and the future is limited to this realm.

Natural —Decisions and plans are without spiritual perception; they are the result of our own natural, distorted reasoning.

Demonic —The events and circumstances of our choices may seem to work out with amazing and coincidental accounts. A diabolical scheme and empowerment seem to accompany the fulfillment of our selfish and corrupt desires.

Our systems actually have two basic motives: to meet needs and to protect us from being hurt again.

Our systems may begin as early as birth and continue its diverse development unless intercepted by the grace of God.

See to it that no one comes short of the grace of God; that no root of bitterness springing up causes trouble, and by it many be defiled. (Hebrews 12:15).

Chapter 4

Reframing—Part II

Replacing Faulty Belief Systems with Truth

Reframing is the ability to perceive situations and events in our mind and emotions by viewing them in a positive and meaningful way. We are able to see the benefits of an experience as we gain God's perspective. Reframing involves looking at life experiences with God's interpretation.

Ways to Reframe our Belief Systems

A. THROUGH THE SCRIPTURES

1. THE WORD OF GOD *IN* US (REVELATION)

Thy word I have treasured in my heart, that I may not sin against Thee. (Psalms 119:11)

I urge you therefore, brethren, by the mercies of God, to present your bodies a living and holy sacrifice, acceptable to God, which is your spiritual service of worship. And do not be conformed to this world, but be transformed by the renewing of your mind, that you may prove what the will of God is, that which is good and acceptable and perfect. (Romans 12:1-2)

2. THE WORD OF GOD *TO* US (ILLUMINATION)

Then they cried out to the Lord in their trouble; He saved them out of their distresses. He sent His word and healed them, and delivered them from their destructions. (Psalms 107:19-20)

For the Word of God is living and active and sharper than any two-edged sword, and piercing as far as the division of soul and spirit, of both joints and marrow, and able to judge the thoughts and intentions of the heart. (Hebrews 4:12)

3. THE WORD OF GOD *THROUGH* US (IMPARTATION)

And Jesus answered saying to them, "Have faith in God. Truly I say to you, whoever says to this mountain, 'Be taken up and cast into the sea,' and does not doubt in his heart, but believes that what he says is going to happen, it shall be granted him.

Therefore I say to you, all things for which you pray and ask, believe that you have received them, and they shall be granted you. (Mark 11:22-24)

For I will not presume to speak of anything except what Christ has accomplished through me, resulting in the obedience of the Gentiles by word and deed, in the power of signs and wonders, in the power of the Spirit. (Romans 15:18-19a)

B. THROUGH ASKING QUESTIONS

Job 38:1 - 42:6

Past events: What character did God build in me through these experiences?

Present circumstances: What is God teaching me now?

Future plans: What is God preparing me for?

C. THROUGH WRITING OR JOURNALING

I will stand on my guard post and station myself on the rampart; and I will keep watch to see what He will speak to me, and how I may reply when I am reproved. The Lord answered me and said, "Record the vision and inscribe it on tablets, that the one who reads it may run. (Habakkuk 2:1-2)

To God or from God

To person or persons offending you

To yourself

D. RESTATING WORDS AND PHRASES

Always vs. sometimes

Words vs. attitude

Word Pictures

E. THROUGH PRAYER AND REVELATION

1. ASK FOR WISDOM

But if any of you lacks wisdom, let him ask of God, who gives to all men generously and without reproach, and it will be given to him. (James 1:5)

2. LISTEN A SECOND TIME

Why do you complain against Him, that He does not give an account of all His doings: Indeed God speaks once, or twice, yet no one notices it. In a dream, a vision of the night, when sound sleep falls on men, while they slumber in their beds, then He opens the ears of men, and seals their instructions, that He may turn aside from his conduct, and keep man from pride; He keeps back his soul from the pit, and his life from passing over into Sheol. (Job 33:13-18)

Renewal in the Spirit Takes Place by Revelation

Activity, understanding, information and discipline apart from the power of the Holy Spirit will not change us in our inner being. It is by the power of the Spirit that renewal occurs.

Definition of revelation: to take the cover off, to reveal.

• Information in the mind (soul) gives understanding.

• Revelation in the spirit results in immediate change

For the bread of God is that which comes down out of heaven and gives life to the world. (John 6:33)

But when He, the Spirit of truth, comes, He will guide you into all truth; for He will not speak on His own initiative, but whatever He hears, He will speak; and He will

disclose to you what is to come. He shall glorify Me; for He shall take of Mine, and shall disclose it to you. All things that the Father has are Mine; therefore I said, that He takes of Mine, and will disclose it to you. (John 16:13-15)

For the mind set on the flesh is death, but the mind set on the Spirit is life and peace. (Romans 8:6)

For to us God revealed them through the Spirit; for the Spirit searches all things, even the depths of God. For who among men knows the thoughts of a man except the spirit of the man, which is in him? Even so the thoughts of God no one knows except the Spirit of God. Now we have received, not the spirit of the world, but the Spirit who is from God, that we might know the things freely given to us by God, which things we also speak, not in works taught by human wisdom, but in those taught by the Spirit, combining spiritual thought with spiritual words. But a natural man does not accept the things of the Spirit of God; for they are foolishness to him, and he cannot understand them, because they are spiritually appraised. But he who is spiritual appraises all things, yet he himself is appraised by no man. For who has known the mind of the Lord, that he should instruct Him? But we have the mind of Christ. (1 Corinthians 2:10-16)

Who also made adequate as servants of a new covenant, not of the letter, but of the Spirit; for the letter kills, but the Spirit gives life. (2 Corinthians 3:6)

INSIGHTS CONCERNING REVELATION

⟨ Will harmonize with the written scriptures; will never violate the character and nature of God.

⟨ Is progressive in man's receiving

⟨ Is diverse in relationship to the needs of the time

⟨ Results in being changed into the image of Christ

A New World View

Unreality results when the immediate and long-term consequences of an action are not considered or comprehended. A person's reframing should involve a new perspective of long range and eternal consequence.

And, although they know the ordinance of God, that those who practice such things are worthy of death, they not only do the same, but also give hearty approval to those who practice them. (Romans 1:32a)

⟨ A wrong appraisal of actions

Wisdom involves the right appraisal of one's actions – both right and wrong.

⟨ The inversion of good and evil

The mental process now calls wrong, right, and that which is right, wrong.

At this stage, the person needing help may not even see the need, or worse, may not even want help.

THE FOLLOWING PRAYER STRATEGY IS SUGGESTED:

1. Pray that the Lord would grant repentance unto life.

2. Pray that the mind-set over the person will be broken by the Holy Spirit to hear the illumination of the truth.

3. Pray that the Lord will bring circumstances into the person's life in order to help expose the unreality of their life-style and give insight into what is reality.

REBONDING - PART 1

Chapter 5

Rebonding—Part I

Learning to Meet Legitimate Needs in Legitimate Ways

When basic legitimate needs are not met, especially during childhood, appropriate bonding may be interrupted, resulting in feelings of loss. Feelings of loss may develop into bitter anger and blame. These emotions often generate negative responses that are directed toward those not fulfilling expectations—even toward God. This tendency is a by product of mans sinful nature. There is a need to release judgements and forgive one's offenders. This opens the door for rebonding and restoration of the soul.

Development of Bitter Judgments

For even though they knew God, they did not honor Him as God, or give thanks; but they became futile in their speculations, and their foolish heart was darkened. (Romans 1:21)

- Did not honor God, judged Him as weak

Judgment is emotionally imprisoning another person as weak, condemning them to a former condition of actions and responses.

> *Do not speak against one another, brethren. He who speaks against a brother, or judges his brother, speaks against the laws and judges the law; but if you judge the law, you are not a doer of the law, but a judge of it. There is only one Lawgiver and Judge, the One who is able to save and to destroy; but who are you who judge your neighbor? (James 4:11-12)*

- Did not give thanks, unfulfilled expectations, resulting in bitterness

Bitterness is a desire to see another hurt for hurting us and is caused by a lack of forgiveness and not responding to God's grace.

> *See to it that no one comes short of the grace of God; that no root of bitterness springing up causes trouble, and by it many be defiled. (Hebrews 12:15)*

When a person has directed their bitter judgements against others, especially God, he will also tend to reject (suppress) the beliefs, the values and the person of the one being judged.

Suppressing the Truth

For the wrath of God is revealed from heaven against all ungodliness and unrighteousness of men, who suppress the truth in unrighteousness, because that which is known about God is evident within them; for God made it evident to them. For since the creation of the world His invisible attributes, His eternal power and divine nature, have been clearly seen, being understood through what has been made, so that they are without excuse. (Romans 1:18-20)

Suppress means to "hold down" the truth. This would be like holding a balloon filled with air under the water

Truth:

1. Evident within them

2. God made it evident to them

3. Clearly seen and understood through what has been made

4. Since the creation of the world

Therefore, this truth can be found within man at the creation

Then God said, "Let Us make man, in Our image, according to Our likeness; and let them rule over the fish of the sea and over the birds of the sky and over the cattle and over all the earth, and over every creeping thing that creeps on the earth. And God created man in His own image, in the image of God He created him; male and female He created them. And God blessed them; and God said to them, "Be fruitful and multiply, and fill the earth, and subdue it; and rule over the fish of the sea and over the birds of the sky, and over every living that that moves on the earth. (Genesis 1:26-28)

As this passage reveals, the creation of man involves three aspects of God

- God's Image

- God's Likeness

- God's Dominion

Creation of Man

A. GOD'S IMAGE (HIS BEING)

- Christ, the last Adam is called the IMAGE of God.

    In whose case the god of this world has blinded the minds of the unbelieving, that they might not see the light of the gospel of the glory of Christ, who is the image of God. (2 Corinthians 4:4)

    And He is the image of the invisible God, the first-born of all creation. For by Him all things were created, both in the heavens and on earth, visible and invisible, whether thrones or dominions or rulers or authorities—all things have been created by Him and for Him. (Colossians 1:15-16)

- This image, into which we are being transformed, is called the GLORY of God.

    For a man ought not to have his head covered, since he is the image and glory of God; but the woman is the glory of man. (1 Corinthians 11:7)

    But we all, with unveiled face beholding as in a mirror the glory of the Lord, are being transformed into the same image from glory to glory, just as from the Lord, the Spirit. (2 Corinthians 3:18)

- The image includes the life and CHARACTER of God.

    Therefore consider the members of your earthly body as dead to immorality, impurity, passion, evil desire, and greed, which amounts to idolatry. For it is on account of these things that the wrath of God will come, and in them you also once walked, when you were living in them. But now you also, put them all aside: anger, wrath, malice, slander, and abusive speech from your mouth. Do not lie to one another, since you laid aside the old self with its evil practices, and have put on the new self who is being renewed to a true knowledge according to the image of the One who created him. (Colossians 3:5-10)

Therefore, God's IMAGE includes His CHARACTER and His GLORY.

B. GOD'S LIKENESS (HIS ORDER)

- Male and female

- Our being in God's likeness involves relationships, the need for fellowship and belonging.

- Jesus recognized this thirst for relationship with man when he invited man to come to Him to fill that thirst.

> *Now on the last day, the great day of the feast, Jesus stood and cried out, saying, "If any man is thirsty, let him come to Me and drink. He who believes in Me, as the Scriptures said, 'From his innermost being shall flow rivers of living water.'"(John 7:37-38)*

C. GOD'S DOMINION (HIS PURPOSE)

Man's need for significance as to purpose and calling in life fills this need. However, outside of Gods will, this drive becomes self-seeking and destructive.

- Be Fruitful   Principles of fruitfulness (John 15)

- Multiply   Principles of increase (2 Peter 1)

- Fill the Earth   Principles of discipleship (2 Timothy 2)

- Subdue it   Principles of warfare (Ephesians 6)

- Rule Over   Principles of divine order (Ephesians 4)

Any violation of these three areas—God's image, likeness or dominion—results in suppressing the truth of God in us or in others.

God's Purpose in the Gospel

> *For I am not ashamed of the gospel, for it is the power of God for salvation to every one who believes, to the Jew first and also to the Greek. For in it the righteousness of God is revealed from faith to faith; as it is written, "But the righteous man shall live by faith." (Romans 1:16-17)*

Even though man fell short of God's plan, His desire and purpose is to redeem us and restore us to wholeness—in spirit, soul and body.

> *Now may the God of peace Himself sanctify you entirely; and may your spirit and soul and body be preserved complete, without blame at the coming of our Lord Jesus Christ. Faithful is He who calls you, and He also will bring it to pass. (1 Thessalonians 5:23-24)*

A. SPIRITUAL DEVELOPMENT

Man has a need for spiritual rebirth. The process of man's spiritual growth and maturity involves being transformed into God's image, likeness and dominion.

> *I am writing to you, little children, because your sins are forgiven you for His name's sake. I am writing to you, fathers, because you know Him who has been from the beginning. I am writing to you, young men, because you have overcome the evil one. I have written to you, children, because you know the Father. I have written to you, fathers, because you know Him who has been from the beginning. I have written to you, young men, because you are strong, and the word of God abides in you, and you have overcome the evil one. (1 John 2:12-14)*

B. PHYSICAL DEVELOPMENT

Man's physical growth process is by God's design:

⟨   Development in the womb

> *For Thou didst form my inward parts; Thou didst weave me in my mother's womb. I will give thanks to Thee, for I am fearfully and wonderfully made; wonderful are Thy works, and my soul knows it very well. My frame was not hidden from Thee, when I was made in secret, and skillfully wrought in the depths of the earth. Thine eyes have seen my unformed substance; and in Thy book they were all written, the days that were ordained for me, when as yet there was not one of them. (Psalm 139:13-16)*

⟨   Development of bone structure, motor skills, natural senses, etc.

C. PSYCHOLOGICAL DEVELOPMENT

Man's psychological and soul development was intended to be in conformity with God's design for man's wholeness. This aspect has sometimes been neglected or seen as unimportant—even worse, as evil and unrelated to our spirituality. On the contrary, our psychological and emotional being is also to be transformed into the image of Christ.

> *I urge you therefore, brethren, by the mercies of God, to present your bodies a living and holy sacrifice, acceptable to God, which is your spiritual service of worship. And do not be conformed to this world, but be transformed by the renewing of your mind, that you may prove what is good and acceptable and perfect. (Romans 12:1-2)*

> *Therefore putting aside all filthiness and all that remains of wickedness, in humility receive the word implanted, which is able to save your souls. (James 1:21)*

Though our soul is not born again as our spirit is, the soul needs to be transformed. The soul includes our mind, will and emotions. These areas of our personality are not suddenly transformed when we initially become a Christian; thus, we often bring unnecessary "baggage" into the Christian life. These areas (mind, will and emotions) have often been sabotaged and need to be restored

Our Psychological Development

A. GOD'S LIKENESS (OUR SENSE OF BEING)

From ages birth to three, we develop our sense of being.

Basic Needs:
Total trust–Nurturing, unconditional love
Touch, warmth
Dependency, eating, being taken care of
Setting boundaries (healthy shame and unhealthy shame)
Curiosity
To explore and do

How unmet:
Self image comes from the face of the one taking care:
You don't exist
You are unimportant
Your birth was not wanted
We wanted a child of the other sex
Hurry up
Unrealistic expectations from parent

Possible Problems:
Addict (drug, alcohol, sex)
Obesity
Emotional dependency
Performance orientation
Doing what others want
Lack of creativity
Fear of taking initiative

⟨ **FULFILLED IN RELATIONSHIP TO GOD THE FATHER**

⟨ **RESTORATIVE RELATIONSHIP—REPARENTING**

B. GOD'S IMAGE (OUR SENSE OF BELONGING)

During ages three to seven, a child develops his or her sense of belonging and identity, and sense of order.

Basic Needs: Gender identity—affirmation
Testing of power
Social relationships (who am I?)

How unmet: Lack of bonding with either parent
Abuse—sexual, physical or emotional
Turning nurturing needs into sexual interest
Curiosity and experimentation

Possible Problems:
Lack of proper identity
Seeking mothering or fathering through sexual contacts
Lack of boundaries
Lack of proper authority in personal life

⟨   **FULFILLED IN RELATIONSHIP TO JESUS CHRIST**

⟨   **RESTORATIVE RELATIONSHIP—COMRADE**

C. GOD'S DOMINION (OUR SENSE OF BECOMING)

Ages seven to twelve, a child learns how to learn. It begins experiencing a sense of purpose and learns skills for the future.

Basic Needs: Competence
Learning how to learn
Development of skills
Learning to think logically

How unmet: Lack of modeling
Abandonment (parent not there for child)

Possible Problems: Inferiority complex
Passivity

Overachiever or over-organizer

⟨　**FULFILLED IN RELATIONSHIP THE HOLY SPIRIT**

⟨　**RESTORATIVE RELATIONSHIP—MENTOR OR COACH**

Emotional Arrest
When we are tramatized in life experiences, we may become emotionally arrested or "stuck."

Reparative Drives
When these needs are not me we will tend to meet them in illegitimate ways by attaching them to something or someone.
In man's fallen and unredeemed state, the basic needs of our being, belonging and becoming are still valid. Man without the Holy Spirit will attempt to meet these basic needs in his own way. The search for bonding and meaningful relationships to fill these unmet needs may be attached to any number of people, things or processes. Thus, the need for appropriate bonding is, indeed, one of the necessary steps to freedom and wholeness.

(Refer to pages 29 and 30)

God's image—our sense of being

Basic need:　Nurturing

God's likeness—our sense of belonging

Basic need:　Affirmation of gender identity

God's dominion—our Sense of becoming
Basic need:　Competence

Chapter 6

Rebonding – Part II

Replacing Wrong Relationships with Healthy Relationships

Rebonding involves giving God our whole heart and committing ourselves to those to whom He has committed us. As we come out of unhealthy relationships and various addictions, there is a need for healthy rebonding to occur. We must be reunited in our hearts to God and appropriately connected to the body of Christ.

What is Bonding?

A bond is that which binds, fastens and holds together. As people enter into relationship, there occurs a binding together of their lives at some level. Bonding involves the ability to establish an emotional attachment to another person. It allows us to relate to others on the deepest levels. With healthy bonding comes the freedom to share dreams, feelings, and deepest thoughts without the fear of rejection by the other person. This type of bonding is normal and right. Yet, as we engage in unhealthy relationships, we become inappropriately bonded. We experience the pull from another person; we feel scattered and fragmented, unable to experience the joy of the Lord. In this chapter, we will look at some of the types of inappropriate and appropriate bonding.

Types of Inappropriate Soul Bonding

- Immoral relationships

- Dependent emotional relationships

- Enmeshed family relationships

- Unresolved grief because of death of separation

- Unforgiveness

- Vows, devotion and commitments to idols, Satan and demons

- Blind and unwavering loyalty to an institution, organization, denomination, etc.

WHEN INAPPROPRIATE SOUL BONDING HAS OCCURRED THE FOLLOWING PRAYERS ARE RECOMMENDED:

1. **ASK GOD TO UNITE OUR HEART** thus freeing us from all inappropriate soul ties.

   Teach me Thy way, O Lord: I will walk in Thy truth; unite my heart to fear Thy name. (Psalm 86:22)

2. **GIVE OUR WHOLE HEART TO GOD** and sanctify Christ as Lord in every area of our life.

   Surely goodness and lovingkindness will follow me all the days of my life, and I will dwell in the house of the Lord forever. (Psalms 23:6)

   But sanctify Christ as Lord in you hearts, always being ready to make a defense to everyone who asks you to give and account for the hope that is in you, yet with gentleness and reverence. (1 Peter 3:15)

3. **ASK GOD TO COMMIT US** to those to whom He has committed us (God's kingdom, family, friends, occupation, etc.)

   For this reason, when I could endure it no longer, I also sent to find out about your faith, for fear that the tempter might have tempted you, and our labor should be in vain. (1 Thessalonians 3:4)

   For it is only right for me to feel this way about you all, because I have you in my heart, since both in my imprisonment and in the defense and confirmation of the gospel, you all are partakers of grace with me. (Philippians 1:7)

   And convinced of this, I know that I shall remain and continue with you all for your progress and joy in the faith. (Philippians 1:25)

4. **GIVE ALL EXPECTATIONS** and ultimate approval needs to God.

   My soul, wait in silence for God only, for my hope is from Him. (Psalms 62:1)

REBONDING - PART 2

Types of Appropriate Bonding

A. FELLOWSHIP

We first establish fellowship with the Lord and then with others (1 John 1:7) Fellowship occurs when the spirit of Christ in one person touches and communicates with the spirit of Christ in another person. The spirit of Christ, in union with our human spirit, is able to respond without measure, dependent or course, upon one's sensitivity, discernment, and anointing. In this sense, we can bond in the spirit with any individual believer or a group of believers.

LEVELS OF FELLOWSHIP

1. FELLOW BELIEVERS—the early church

And they were continually devoting themselves to the apostles' teaching and to fellowship, to the breaking of bread and to prayer. (Acts 2:42)

2. FELLOW LABORERS IN MINISTRY—Paul and Barnabas

Just as you learned it from Epaphras, our beloved fellow bond-servant, who is a faithful servant of Christ on our behalf. (Colossians 1:7)

But I thought it necessary to send to you Epaphroditus, my brother and fellow worker and fellow soldier, who is also you messenger and minister to my need. (Philippians 2:25)

3. SPIRITUAL SON OR DAUGHTER – Paul and Timothy

But I hope in the Lord Jesus to send Timothy to you shortly, so that I also my be encouraged when I learn of your condition. For I have no one else of kindred spirit who will genuinely be concerned for your welfare. For they all seek after their own interests, not those of Christ Jesus (Philippians 2:19-22)

B.   **FRIENDSHIP**

SOUL—Jonathan and David

Now it came about when he had finished speaking to Saul, that the soul of Jonathan was knit to the soul of David, and Jonathan loved him as himself. And Saul took him that day and did not let him return to his father's house. Then Jonathan made a covenant with David because he loved him as himself. And Jonathan stripped himself of the robe that was on him and gave it to David, with his armor, including his sword and his bow and his belt. (1 Samuel 18:1-4)

Friendship occurs when expressions of our soul (mind, will and emotions) connect and relate to those of another. Thus, bonding can take place at various limited, guarded or intimate levels:

1. **THE MIND OR INTELLECT**—Having common intellectual interests. Friendship or bonding at this level usually involves commonality in realms of mutual agreement, such as politics, religion, world events, social and moral issues, etc.

2. **THE WILL OR VOLITION**—Participating in common activities. Friendship or bonding at this level goes further than simply sharing intellectual interests. It involves doing things together, spending time on common interests and making decisions that affect each other.

3. **EMOTIONS AND FEELINGS**—Sharing feelings and emotional needs. Deeper levels of bonding and friendship occur when both people begin to share feelings, needs, histories and intimate details of their lives.

The healthiest bonding takes place progressively, beginning with spiritual oneness, and develops with time.

C. **COMRADESHIP**

Comradeship is a bonding together and commitment for ministry. It seems that God first calls people together in relationships before he calls them together in ministry. This seems to have been his own pattern with the twelve disciples. It was also evident in the New Testament order among the early leaders, such as Paul and Barnabas, and Peter and John.

The knitting together of the souls of David and Jonathan is probably one of the best examples of comradeship. This type of friendship is perhaps the one most men desire but never achieve.

D. COMPANIONSHIP

Marriage without bonding at all these levels, including the expression of sexual intimacy, is in reality only a mirage of what God really intended. When a marriage is based only on emotional and physical intimacy, true bonding is interrupted by the lack of spiritual development and friendship. Conversely, marriage including spiritual oneness and friendship but lacking physical and sexual intimacy may also lack the deepest expressions of closeness and intimacy.

Bonding Priorities

1. RELATIONSHIP WITH GOD THE FATHER THROUGH JESUS CHRIST

But if we walk in the light as He Himself is in the light, we have fellowship with one another, and the blood of Jesus His Son cleanses us from all sin. (1 John 1:7)

This mystery is great; but I am speaking with reference to Christ and the church. (Ephesians 5:32).

Father, I desire that they also, whom Thou hast given Me, be with Me where I am, in order that they may behold My glory, which Thou hast given Me; for Thou didst love Me before the foundation of the world...and I have made Thy name known to them, and will make it known; that the love wherewith Thou didst love Me may be in them, and I in them. (John 17:24, 26)

2. RELATIONSHIP WITH OUR FAMILY

"Husbands, love your wives, just as Christ loved the church and gave Himself up for her" (Ephesians 5:25).

"So husbands ought also to love their own wives as their own bodies. He who loves his wife loves himself" (Ephesians 5:28).

Hindrances to Bonding

One of the deepest longings of the human heart is to be in a meaningful relationship with another person. This longing is often never fulfilled because of hindrances that sabotage the bonding process. True bonding will occur only as these hindrances are removed. The three most prevalent hindrances to bonding are:

⟨ **FEAR OF REJECTION**

⟨ **LACK OF FORGIVENESS**

⟨ **POSSESSIVENESS**

Twelve Steps to Bonding

1. **TAKE THE INITIATIVE.**

2. **RISK VULNERABILITY.**

3. **LEARN ABOUT THE INTERESTS OF OTHERS.**

4. **EXPRESS GRATITUDE AND APPRECIATION.**

5. **SHOW RESPECT.**

6. ALLOW FOR SHORTCOMINGS.

7. SHARE BLIND SPOTS.

8. EXPERIENCE THE POWER OF TOUCH.

9. LEARN TO BLESS OTHERS.

10. DEVELOP LOYALTY & TRUST.

11. GIVE A RELATIONSHIP SPACE.

12. HELP FULFILL ANOTHER'S GOAL & CALLING IN LIFE.

Chapter 7

Reanchoring–Part I

Replacing Immature Human Response with God's Wisdom

The difference between childishness and mature responses is the order of responding. A child speaks and acts before he or she thinks and reasons. It is often true in our adult lives that we still act out of our childish responses. At first thought, these systems of responses may seem harmless; however, we soon find that if we don't learn to respond to difficult life situations in mature ways, we may end up in a shipwreck in our personal life, our relationships and our jobs.

> *When I was a child, I used to speak as a child, think as a child, reason as a child; when I became a man, I did away with childish things. (1 Corinthians 13:11)*

Reasons for Immature Responses

A. WOUNDEDNESS

WOUNDED PEOPLE WOUND PEOPLE

When the relationship affecting our spiritual and emotional growth are interrupted through overt or covert activities, a wall is built and the relationship is hindered or sabotaged. Additional hurts from others may reinforce this wall, preventing further relationships and hindering growth. Often feelings of hurt or offense are also transferred toward God, causing isolation and loneliness. Below is a list of three common wounded personality types and their characteristics.

Sometimes another person may serve as a role model to reflect God's character and love; however, there may be guarded reception resulting in limited and selective relationships.

Ultimately, healing and restoration will involve forgiving those who have hurt us. Removing the walls and barriers to these relationships does not mean they must be exactly the same as before, rather the restored relationship may have new boundaries and definitions, limits, etc.

⟨ Walls

A brother offended is harder to be won than a strong city, and contentions are like the bars of a castle. (Proverbs 18:19)

⟨ Permanent, unmovable

⟨ Isolates and shuts out

⟨ Motivated by fear–"I will not be hurt again"

⟨ Boundaries

The Lord will tear down the house of proud, but He will establish the boundary of the widow. (Proverbs 15:25)

⟨ Sets limits, can be changed

⟨ Protects and defines

⟨ Motivated by love–"I want God's best for myself and others."

1. WOUNDED PERSONALITY

⟨ Builds a wall of hurt to protect from further hurt.

⟨ Isolation and loneliness

⟨ Hardness and coldness of heart

2. A TRAUMATIZED PERSONALITY

⟨ Total or partial loss of memory, especially childhood
A person who has been severely traumatized through abuse and molestation (physical, sexual and emotional) may close himself off through loss of memories in an attempt to eliminate pain.

⟨ Deep sense of shame and self hate

⟨ Distrust of others

⟨ Fear of abandonment

3. A FRAGMENTED PERSONALITY

⟨ The arresting of personality growth may occur in one specific area (such as: self image, relationship, or life purpose). Other areas will also be affected, but not to the same degree.

⟨ Compartmentalizing experiences and perceptions

⟨ Feelings of being fragmented and splintered in most effected area

⟨ Instability of behavior and emotions

⟨ May be expressed through different personality types

A. LEARNED FAMILY BEHAVIOR

Many of our responses to life situations, especially to pressure and stress, were learned from family examples.

1. How did your family respond to stress?

2. How did your family respond to offenses?

3. How did your family respond to loss?

But if you bite and devour one another, take care lest you be consumed by one another. (Galatians 5:15)

See to it that no one comes short of the grace of God; that no root of bitterness springing up causes trouble, and by it many be defiled. (Hebrews 12:15)

The Lord is slow to anger and abundant in loving-kindness, forgiving iniquity and transgression; but He will by no means clear the guilty, visiting the iniquity of the fathers on the children to the third and fourth generations. (Numbers 14:18)

REANCHORING · PART 1

A. SELFISH AMBITION WITH DISREGARD FOR GOD'S KINGDOM AND OTHERS

*For where jealousy and selfish ambition exist, there is disorder and every evil thing.
(James 3:16)*

THE DEVELOPMENT OF SELFISH AMBITION

*And with all deception of wickedness for those who perish, because they did not
receive the love of the truth so as to be saved. And for this reason God will send
upon them a deluding influence so that they might believe what is false, in order that
they all may be judged who did not believe the truth, but took pleasure in wickedness.
(2 Thessalonians 2:10-12)*

1. "THEY DID NOT RECEIVE THE LOVE OF THE TRUTH..."

When we rejected God's image, God's likeness and God's dominion as the
design for our life, we rejected God's love as well as the opportunity to be a
channel of His love to others.

2. THEY BELIEVED WHAT IS FALSE..."

Our rejection of God's design was the result of our unbelief. Not believing
God, we didn't follow His plan for us. We devised our own false way to
meet our needs and live our life.

3. THEY TOOK PLEASURE IN WICKEDNESS ..."

Our false way included a choice that would be pleasurable.

When selfish ambition is fully developed, it parallels the five "I wills" of
Satan and it becomes iniquity drives.

*But you said in your heart,
I will raise my throne above the stars of God,
I will sit on the mount of assembly in the recesses of the north
I will ascend above the heights of the clouds;
I will make myself like the Most High." (Isaiah 14:13-14)*

43

REANCHORING · PART 1

The Iniquity Drives

Motivation	"I Will" Statements of Satan Isaiah 14:12-14	Iniquity Drives Of Human Beings
Self Righteousness	"I will ascend to heaven."	The human drives to be accepted on the basis of our good works. We feel that approval is based on performance.
Self-Exaltation	"I will raise my throne above the stars of God."	We strive to bring honor and glory to self. We want to be looked up to by others.
Self-Appointment	"I will sit on the mount of assembly in the recesses of the north."	We desire to belong. We will promote ourselves without regard for the ministry and abilities of others.
Self-Display	"I will ascend above the heights of the clouds."	We seek to be recognized for our personal achievements. We may even want to be idolized.
Self-sustaining	"I will make myself like the Most High."	We want to be independent and self-sufficient. We view being dependent on people as being controlled by them.

Iniquity drives are dealt with through the process of travail and repentance.

Travail

As a result of the anguish of His soul, He will see it and be satisfied; by His knowledge the Righteous One, My Servant, will justify the many as He will bear their iniquities. (Isaiah 53:11)

Repentance

Search me, O god, and know my heart; Try me and know my anxious thoughts. (Psalms 139:23)

A. REPETITIVE & COMPULSIVE BEHAVIOR

Habitual responses result in compulsive/addictive behaviors. Though most addictive behaviors are multiple and generational, each person is responsible for their own irresponsible choices.

1. INTRODUCTION

⟨   Availability

⟨   Experimentation

⟨   Initial feelings

2. CONTINUANCE OF EXPERIMENTATION

⟨   Seeks to feel initial feelings

⟨   Fantasy becomes a part of seeking (getting there is part of the high).

3. OBSESSION

⟨   High from addiction is considered the norm.

⟨   Experiences difficulty in feeling the initial feeling all the time

4. CONSUMING

⟨   The addiction becomes the most important thing in a person's life.

5. DISTORTION OF REALITY OCCURS

For we know that the Law is spiritual; but I am of flesh, sold into bondage to sin.
For that which I am doing, I do not understand; for I am not practicing what I

would like to do, but I am doing the very thing I hate. But if I do the very thing I do not wish to do, I agree with the Law, confessing that it is good. So now, no longer am I the one doing it, but sin which indwells me. For I know that nothing good dwells in me, that is, in my flesh; for the wishing is present in me, but the doing of the good is not. For the good that I wish, I do not do; but I practice the very evil that I do not wish. But if I am doing the very thing I do not wish, I am no longer doing it, but sin which dwells in me. I find then the principle that evil is present in me, the one who wishes to do good. For I joyfully concur with the law of God in the inner man, but I see a different law in the members of my body, waging war against the law of my mind, and making me a prisoner of the law of sin which is in my members. Wretched man that I am! Who will set me free from the body of this death? (Romans 7:14-24)

The difference between a "strong desire" and an "addiction" is the power of choice. Every person must assume the responsibility for wrong choices, but the addicted person feels beyond choice, especially to say, "no." When we recognize our powerlessness over our addiction, become poor in spirit, and turn to God through Christ, we can become whole.

Chapter 8

Reanchoring–Part II

*Replacing Immature Responses to Difficult Life Circumstances
through Forgiveness, Christlike Responses and New Experiences*

Wounds and painful memories often become negative anchors in our soul that keep us emotionally stuck. Since our responses are often out of these wounds and memories, it is necessary to heal them and replace them with positive anchors of hope in Christ.

This is the hope we have as an anchor of the soul, a hope both sure and steadfast and one which enters within the veil. (Hebrews 6:19)

Releasing Sorrow and Fully Forgiving

Sorrow is the feeling of loss:

This I say therefore, and affirm together with the Lord, that you walk no longer just as the Gentiles also walk, in the futility of their mind, being darkened in their understanding, excluded from the life of God, because of the hardness of their heart; and they, having become callous, have given themselves over to sensuality, for the practice of every kind of impurity with greediness. But you did not learn Christ in this way, if indeed you have heard Him and have been taught in Him just as truth is in Jesus, that, in reference to your former manner of life, you lay aside the old self, which is being corrupted in accordance with the lusts of deceit, and that you be renewed in the spirit of your mind, and put on the new self, which in the likeness of God has be created in righteousness and holiness of truth. (Ephesians 4:17-24)

A. THREE MAJOR CAUSES OF SORROW

1. LOSS OF WELL-BEING (GOD'S IMAGE)

⟨ Physical rejection

⟨ Childhood trauma-abuse

⟨ Comparison with others

⟨ A loss of childhood

2. LOSS OF RELATIONSHIPS (GOD'S LIKENESS)

⟨ Parents (death, divorce, separation)

⟨ Friends (moved, betrayed, death, etc.)

⟨ Spouse (divorce, death, etc.)

⟨ Church division

⟨ God (guilt, believing our prayers are unanswered, etc.)

3. LOSS OF PURPOSE (GOD'S DOMINION)

⟨ Job loss

⟨ Financial loss

⟨ Health restrictions (sickness, accident, aging)

⟨ Non-advancement

We have a need for closure—all of life includes periods of saying "Good-bye." When our grief is not dealt with, the following results may occur:

1. EMOTIONAL

⟨ Unless we deal with the pain and grief of past hurts, we are unable to fully appreciate the love that was expressed.

⟨ Childhood losses not dealt with often become our basis of responding in adult life out of their past hurts.

⟨ Addictions

2. PHYSICAL

If we do not complete the grieving process, physical problems may occur:

⟨ Stomach problems

⟨ Allergies

⟨ Stress

⟨ Lowered immune system

3. SPIRITUAL

⟨ A sense of incompleteness and inability to mature if we are "stuck" in childhood hurts

⟨ Unforgiveness of past offense against us results in distrust of others as well as God.

⟨ Worldly sorrow produces death.

A. UNHEALTHY WAYS OF GRIEVING OUR SORROWS

⟨ Lived in through closing down emotionally

⟨ Lived out through anger, rage, rebellion, etc.

B. TWO KINDS OF SORROW

The sorrow that is according to the will of God produces a repentance without regret, leading to salvation; but the sorrow of the world produces death.

> *For the sorrow that is according to the will of God produces repentance without regret, leading to salvation; but the sorrow of the world produces death. (2 Corinthians 7:10)*

Godly Sorrow (2 Samuel 12:1-14)	Sorrow of the World
A sorrow over the loss of God's glory	A sorrow over personal loss only
Loss of God's glory for others	A resentment or blaming of others
Personal loss of God's glory	Self-pity
Circumstances viewed with God's grace and purpose	Circumstances viewed without a sense of God's grace and purpose

A. RECEIVING AND GIVING FORGIVENESS

Godly sorrow produces repentance and results in receiving God's forgiveness

> *If we confess our sins, He is faithful and righteous to forgive us our sins and to cleanse us from all unrighteousness. (1 John 1:9)*

> *For the sorrow that is according to the will of God produces repentance without regret, leading to salvation; but the sorrow of the world produces death. For behold what earnestness this very thing, this godly sorrow, has produced in you: What vindication of yourselves, what indignation, what fear, what longing, what zeal, what avenging of wrong! In everything you demonstrated yourselves to be innocent in the matter. (2 Corinthians 7:10-11)*

Godly sorrow is anything that breaks the heart of God:

〈   God's heart is broken over sins against Him

〈   God's heart is broken over sins against others.

⟨   God's heart is broken over sins against us.

RESULTS OF GODLY SORROW AN REPENTANCE

For behold what earnestness this very thing, this godly sorrow, has produced in you: What vindication of yourselves, what indignation, what fear, what longing, what zeal, what avenging of wrong! In everything you demonstrated yourselves to be innocent in the matter. (2 Corinthians 7:11)

1. Vindication—New desire and actions to correct past wrong behavior and establish a new credibility and testimony

2. Indignation—There will be a new hatred of sin when we have seen what the results of our behavior and sin. This hatred is not a raging attitude, especially against someone, but a deep sense of repugnancy and turning aside from the sin.

3. Fear—There will be a new awareness of God's presence and sovereignty. We look at life from the aspect of eternity and what is lasting. This fear is a godly sense of loss for the Kingdom.

4. Longing—There will be a desire to fill the vacuum in our soul with His love. Before, we lived out a drive to meet our needs. Now, we have a new passion for Christ and His glory.

5. Zeal—A new level of energy and focus. One who is focused on his own emotional needs will soon lack energy. Emotion is energy in action. It takes energy to be angry, fearful and bitter. As we become free from our struggles and bondage, there is a new zeal and energy for the things of God.

6. Justice—A new sensitivity toward injustice and the power of sin. Often ministries will come out of our failures. When there is a clear conscience, there will be a new desire to free others from the bondage that held us.

The sorrow of the world results in death unless there is repentence and full forgiveness of the offender.

Stages of Forgiveness

And be kind to one another, tender-hearted, forgiving each other, just as God in Christ also has forgiven you. (Ephesians 4:32)

Forgiveness is being released from negative attitudes and fully forgiving from the heart.

1. **RECOGNIZE YOUR FEELINGS** (The prophetical ministry Jesus)

   ⟨   Acknowledge them

   ⟨   Don't minimize them

   ⟨   Let them be as deep as they need to be

   ⟨   Feel them

2. **SHARE YOUR FEELINGS** (The priestly of Jesus)

   ⟨   With Christ

   Since then we have a great high priest who has passed through the heavens, Jesus the Son of God, let us hold fast our confession. For we do not have a high priest who cannot sympathize with our weaknesses, but One who has been tempted in all things as we are, yet without sin. Let us therefore draw near with confidence to the throne of grace, that we may receive mercy and may find grace to help in time of need. (Hebrews 4:14-16)

   ⟨   With others

   Therefore, confess your sins to one another, and pray for one another, so that you may be healed. The effective prayer of a righteous man can accomplish much. (James 5:16)

   To sum up, let all be harmonious, sympathetic, brotherly, kindhearted, and humble in spirit. (I Peter 3:8)

3. MAKE A DECISION (The kingly ministry of Jesus)

A. INSIGHTS INTO FORGIVENESS

Then Peter came and said to Him, "Lord, how often shall my brother sin against me and I forgive him? Up to seven times?"
Jesus said to him, "I do not say to you, up to seven times, but up to seventy times seven. For this reason the kingdom of heaven may be compared to a certain king who wished to settle accounts with his slaves. And when he had begun to settle them, there was brought to him one who owed him ten thousand talents. But since he did not have the means to repay, his lord commanded him to be sold, along with his wife and children and all the he had, and repayment to be made. But the slave therefore falling down, prostrated himself before him, saying, 'Have patience with me, and I will repay you everything.' And the lord of that slave felt compassion and released him and forgave him the debt."
(Matthew 18:21-26)

⟨ Had compassion

⟨ Released from prison

⟨ Forgave debt

B. ADDITIONAL INSIGHTS

1. GIVE EXPECTATIONS TO GOD

My soul, wait in silence for God only, for my hope is from Him. (Psalms 62:5)

2. EXPRESS GRATITUDE FOR HOW GOD WILL USE OFFENSES FOR YOUR BENEFIT AND HIS GLORY.

In the same way the Spirit also helps our weakness; for we do not know how to pray as we should but the Spirit Himself intercedes for us with groanings too deep for words; and He who searches the hearts knows what the mind of the Spirit is, according to the will of God. And we know that God causes all things to work together for good to those who love God, to those who are called according to His purpose. For whom He foreknew, He also predestined to become conformed to the image of His Son, that He might be the first-born among many brethren; and whom He predestined, these He also called: and whom He called, these He also justifies; and whom He justified, these He also glorified. What then shall we say to there things? If God is for us, who is against us? He who did not spare His own Son, but delivered Him up for us all, how will He not also with Him freely give us all

things? Who will bring a charge against God's elect? God is the one who justifies: who is the one who condemns? Christ Jesus is He who dies, yes, rather who was raised, who is at the right hand of God, who also intercedes for us. Who shall separate us from the love of Christ? Shall tribulation, or distress, or persecution, or famine, or nakedness, or peril, or sword? Just as it is written, "For Thy sake we are being put to death all day long; we are considered as sheep to be slaughtered." But in all these things we overwhelmingly conquer through Him who loved us. For I am convinced that neither death, nor life, nor angels, nor principalities, nor things present, nor things to come, nor powers, not height, nor depth, nor any other created thing, shall be able to separate us from the love of God, which is in Christ Jesus our Lord. (Romans 8:26-39)

3. PRAY FOR THE OFFENDER AND PURPOSE TO BLESS THEM IF, AND WHEN, THE OCCASION MAY ARISE.

But I say to you who hear, love your enemies, do good to those who hate you, bless those who curse you, pray for those who mistreat you. (Luke 6:27-28)

Not returning evil for evil, or insult for insult, but giving a blessing instead; for you were called for the very purpose that you might inherit a blessing. (1 Peter 3:9)

4. ASK GOD FOR WISDOM

Consider is all joy, my brethren, when you encounter various trials, knowing that the testing of your faith produces endurance. And let endurance have its perfect result, that you may be perfect and complete, lacking in nothing. But if any of you lacks wisdom, let him ask of God, who gives to all men generously and without reproach, and it will be given to him. (James 1:2-5)

Walking in Wisdom

A. PREPARE TO FACE LIFE SITUATIONS WITH GOD'S WISDOM

1. GIVE NEW VALUE TO A DECISION

Hear, O sons, the instruction of a father, and give attention that you may gain understanding. For I give you sound teaching; do not abandon my instruction. When I was a son to my father, tender and the only son in the sight of my mother, then he taught me and said to me, "Let your heart hold fast my words; keep my commandments and live; acquire wisdom! Acquire understanding! Do not forget, nor turn away from the words of my mouth. "Do not forsake her, and she will guard you; Love her, and she will watch over you. The beginning of wisdom is: Acquire wisdom; and with all your acquiring, get understanding. Prize her, and she will exalt you; she will honor you if you embrace her. She will place on your head a garland of grace; she will present you with a crown of beauty." (Proverbs 4:1-9)

2. MAKE A COMMITMENT TO THE VALUES

Hear, my son, and accept my sayings, and the years of your life will be many. I have directed you in the way of wisdom; I have led you in upright paths. When you walk, your steps will not be impeded; and if you run, you will not stumble. Take hold of instruction; do not let go. Guard her, for she is your life. Do not enter the path of the wicked, and do not proceed in the way of evil men. Avoid it, do not pass by it; turn away from it and pass on. For they cannot sleep unless they do evil; and they are robbed of sleep unless they make someone stumble. For they eat the bread of wickedness, and drink the wine of violence. But the bath of the righteous is like the light of dawn, That shines brighter and brighter until the full day. The way of the wicked is like darkness; they do not know over what they stumble. (Proverbs 4:10-19)

3. REINFORCE THE VALUES AND COMMITMENTS

My son, give attention to my words; incline your ear to my sayings. Do not let them depart from your sight; keep them in the midst of your heart. For they are life to those who find them. And health to their whole body. Watch over your heart with all diligence, for from it flow the springs of life. Put away from you a deceitful mouth, and put devious lips far from you. Let your eyes look directly ahead, and let your gaze be fixed straight in front of you. Watch the path of your feet, and all your ways will be established. Do not turn to the right nor to the left; turn your foot from evil. (Proverbs 4:20-27)

B. LEARN TO WALK IN THE PEACE AND REVELATION OF THE HOLY SPIRIT

Be anxious for nothing, but in everything by prayer and supplication with thanksgiving let your requests be made known to God. And the peace of God, which surpasses all comprehension, shall guard your hearts your minds in Christ Jesus. (Philippians 4:6-7)

C. SEEK COUNSEL FROM OTHERS

Without consultation, plans are frustrated, but with many counselors they succeed. (Proverbs 15:22)

D. CONTINUE TO REPLACE THE OLD ANCHORS OF DISILLUSIONMENT AND HURT THROUGH THE TRANSFORMATION PROCESS

Romance Stage		Disillusionment Stage		Transformation Stage	
___	___	___	___	___	___
___	___	___	___	___	___
___	___	___	___	___	___
___	___	___	___	___	___

Chapter 9

Rebuilding

Replacing Temptations to Fulfill Selfish Ambitions with the Kingdom of God

When boundaries are too lenient or too rigid, they need to be rebuilt. Boundaries are like fences that protect us from intruders, or at the same time, from our going beyond our own responsibilities or limitations.

But we will not boast beyond our measure, but within the measure of the sphere which God apportioned to us as a measure, to reach even as far as you. For we are not overextending ourselves, as if we did not reach to you, for we were the first to come even as far as you in the gospel of Christ. (2 Corinthians 10:13-14)

Understanding Boundaries

A. BOUNDARY IMPAIRMENT

1. NO BOUNDARIES, OR ILL DEFINED BOUNDARIES

2. TOO LENIENT, OR TOO RIGID BOUNDARIES

⟨ Physical

⟨ Emotional

⟨ Sexual

⟨ Spiritual

B. UNDERSTANDING BOUNDARY REBUILDING

1. OUTWARD BOUNDARIES

⟨ A fence that protects

⟨ Landmarks of property ownership

2. INWARD BOUNDARIES (PERSONAL)

⟨ Our sense of responsibilities

⟨ Where our space ends and someone else's begins

⟨ Areas of limitation

- Where we do not go

- Where others do not go

⟨ Basic beliefs and values

⟨ A sense of safety

C. BOUNDARIES ARE GOD GIVEN

Then God said, "Let Us make man in Our image, according to Our likeness; and let them rule over the fish of the sea and over the birds of the sky and over the cattle and over all the earth, and over every creeping thing that creeps on the earth." And God created man in His own image, in the image of God He create him; male and female He created them. And God blessed them; and God said to them, "Be fruitful and multiply, and fill the earth, and subdue it, and rule over the fish of the sea and over the birds of the sky, and over every living thing that moves on the earth." (Genesis 1:26-28)

1. OWNERSHIP

God is Lord of both heaven and earth.

"...Let Us make man...."

2. STEWARDSHIP

Shared God gave steward ship to man

"...Let them rule...."

D. BIBLICAL BASIS FOR BOUNDARIES

1. MORAL BOUNDARIES

(Exodus 20:1-17)

2. GOVERNMENT

Let every person be in subjection to the governing authorities. For there is no authority except from God, and those which exist are established by God. Therefore he who resists authority has opposed the ordinance of God; and they who have opposed will receive condemnation upon themselves. For rulers are not a cause of fear for good behavior, but for evil. Do you want to have no fear of authority? Do what is good, and you will have praise from the same; for it is a minister of God to you for good. But if you do what is evil, be afraid; for it does not bear the sword for nothing; for it is a minister of God, an avenger who brings wrath upon the one who practices evil. Wherefore it is necessary to be in subjection, not only because of wrath, but also for conscience' sake. For because of this you also pay taxes, for rulers are servants of God, devoting themselves to this very thing. Render to all what is due them: tax to whom tax is due; custom to whom custom; fear to whom fear; honor to whom honor. (Romans 13:1-7)

But Peter and John answered and said to them, "Whether it is right in the sight of God to give heed to you rather than to God, you be the judge. (Acts 4:19)

3. MARITAL

Let marriage be held in honor among all and let the marriage bed be undefiled; for fornicators and adulterers God will judge. (Hebrews 13:4)

For this cause a man shall leave his father and his mother, and shall cleave to his wife; and they shall become one flesh. (Genesis 2:24)

(1 Corinthians 7)

4. APPLICATION OF ORDINANCES AND LAWS FOR THE EARLY GENTILE CHURCH

Since we have heard that some of our number to whom we gave no instruction have disturbed you with their words, unsettling your soul, it seemed good to us, having become of one mind, to select men to send to you with our beloved Barnabas and Paul, men who have risked their lives for the name of our Lord Jesus Christ. Therefore we have sent Judas and Silas, who themselves will also report the same thing by word of mouth. For it seemed good to the Holy Spirit and to us to lay upon you no greater burden than these essentials: that you abstain from things sacrificed

to idols and from blood and from things strangled and from fornication; if you keep yourselves free from such things, you will do well. (Acts 15:24-29)

5. GOD ORDAINED

The God who made the world and all things in it, since He is Lord of Heaven and earth, does not dwell in temples made with hands; neither is He served by human hands, as though He needed anything, since He Himself gives to all life and breath and all thing; and He made from one, every nation of mankind to live on all the face of the earth, having determined their appointed times, and the boundaries of their habitations, that they should seek God, if perhaps they might grope for Him and find Him, although He is not far from each one of us. (Acts 17: 24-27)

Characteristics of Healthy Boundaries

⟨ An empowerment to say "no" when others expect "yes"

⟨ Assuming responsibilities for what is ours

⟨ Develops ability to negotiate

⟨ Understands the difference between being "nice" and being "used"

⟨ Establishes a standard of priorities

⟨ Deals with criticisms and accusations in a healthy way

⟨ Establishes a strong sense of morals and ethics

Enemies and Intruders of Boundaries

A. UNHEALTHY SHAME

B. FEAR OR DISAPPROVAL AND ABANDONMENT

C. GUILT

Rebuilding of Boundaries

1. ESTABLISHED BY THE WORD OF GOD

2. ESTABLISHED BY LEGITIMATE DELEGATED AUTHORITY

⟨ Define your personal responsibilities with delegated authority

⟨ Ministry/job vs. family responsibilities

⟨ Work Schedule

3. ESTABLISHED BY PRAYER AND REVELATION

⟨ Devotional

⟨ Personal Ministry

⟨ Giving

B. FOUR WAYS TO STRENGTHEN BOUNDARIES

1. REDEFINE BOUNDARIES AND EXPECTATIONS.

2. PLACE BOUNDARIES UNDER THE LORDSHIP OF CHRIST.

3. LEARN HOW TO PROTECT BOUNDARIES FROM OTHERS.

4. HAVE A SUPPORT SYSTEM TO HELP KEEP BOUNDARIES.

Maintaining and Rebuilding Boundaries in Times of Crisis

Maintaining and rebuilding life's boundaries involves defining boundaries according to God's will and standards.

A. THE CRISIS OF NEED

False core belief: "If God doesn't meet my needs now, on my terms, or in my way, then I cannot trust Him. I will take control of the circumstances myself."

Truth: God is so concerned with our character, attitudes and inward persons, that he may allow circumstances and tests to help bring us to maturity.

> *Consider it all joy, my brethren, when you encounter various trials, knowing that the testing of your faith produces endurance. And let endurance have its perfect result, that you may be perfect and complete, lacking in nothing. (James 1:2-4)*

B. THE CRISIS OF CONSCIENCE

False core belief: "If I make one mistake or have a temptation, or even begin the process of acting out my temptation, then it is proof that I am basically a bad person. I might as well continue in sin. What's the use?"

Truth: It is always beneficial to resist the devil and to immediately stop acting out our temptation. To continue will only bring further ruin or death. Humbling ourselves and acknowledging our need for help will result in receiving the grace and power to overcome.

> *But He gives a greater grace. Therefore it says, "God is opposed to the proud, but gives grace to the humble." Submit therefore to God. Resist the devil and he will flee from you. Draw near to God and He will draw near to you. Cleanse your*

hands, you sinners; and purify your hearts, you double-minded. Be miserable and mourn and weep; let your laughter be turned into mourning, and your joy to gloom. Humble yourselves in the presence of the Lord, and He will exalt you. (James 4:6-10)

C. THE CRISIS OF RELATIONSHIP

False belief: "If others make a mistake or disappoint me, then it only proves that I can't trust them, they will only hurt or betray me again."

Truth: The circumstances of persons, places, and things do not make us happy or unhappy. We choose our emotional state by the way we view live and circumstances. Our judgment and condemnation of others is the rejection of ourselves.

Therefore you are without excuse, every man of you who passes judgment, for in that you judge another, you condemn yourself; for you who judge practice the same things. And we know that the judgment of God rightly falls upon those who practice such things. (Romans 2:1-2)

D. THE CRISIS OF MINISTRY

False belief: "My ministry and purpose in life is not affected by what I do or say as long as others do not know my failures or sins. My private life can be different from my public life."

Truth: My ministry and purpose in life is affected by my private life. Guilt and dishonesty will affect my relationships and ministry to others through deception and manipulation.

But we have renounced the things hidden because of shame, not walking in craftiness or adulterating the word of God, but by the manifestation of truth commending ourselves to every man's conscience in the sight of God. (2 Corinthians 4:2)

Chapter 10

Redirecting Passions

Repositioning Relationships and Plans to Fulfill God's Plan.

Values determine actions. The Lord does not judge the outward man, but the thoughts and intents of the heart (Hebrews 4:12). In Psalm 26:2, David asked the Lord to examine him and to test his mind (reins) and heart.

The "reins" of the heart is used in many passages in scripture and is also translated "mind." It literally means "kidneys" and is equivalent to the usage of the New Testament concept of "bowels" of mercy, tenderness and kindness. In 2 Corinthians 6:12, Paul tells the believers they are restrained by their own affections (bowels).

Therefore, the "reins" of the heart and the "bowels," or affections, refer to the inward parts of our "heart of hearts"—actually, the value and passions of the heart.

Our goals, choices and actions will be based upon our passions and the value system of our heart. That is, we will do what we believe is important and has value to us.

TWO VALUE SYSTEMS:

1. Immature value system

    Based on what will meet our needs (selfish ambition)

2. Mature value system

    Based on what will bring glory to the kingdom of God

A False Value System

Professing to be wise, they became fools, and exchanged the glory of God...(Romans 1:22-23)

A value is anything we consider important. When the scripture speaks of the reigns of our heart, it is speaking of our passions, or value systems. When Jesus said that where a man's treasure there will his heart be also, (Matthew 6:21), He was referring to a person's values. Our values are how we represent something to ourselves. Our values and belief systems determine our behavior.

Professing to be wise, they became fools...(Romans 1:22)

Since a wrong belief system only reinforces our lack of proper identity, one seeks value, identity, purpose and even worship in another person or thing.

And exchanged the glory of the incorruptible God for an image in the form of corruptible man and of birds and four-footed animals and crawling creatures. (Romans 1:23)

DISCERNING OUR VALUE SYSTEM

Therefore be careful how you walk, not as unwise men, but as wise, making the most of your time, because the days are evil. So then do not be foolish, but understand what the will of the Lord is. (Ephesians 5:15-17)

1. What takes priority in our lives?

2. In what do we invest interest, time, finances, etc.?

3. For what will we endure?

4. For what will we live and die?

5. What are the greatest determinants in our decision making?

Replacing a Faulty Value System

A. REDIRECTIONG OUR HEARTS INTO THE WILL OF GOD

As new believers, we receive a new spirit (the Holy Spirit), a new mind (the Mind of the Holy Spirit) and a new heart (a new creation or new man).

> *Moreover, I will give you a new heart and put a new spirit within you; and I will remove the heart of stone from your flesh and give you a heart of flesh. (Ezekiel 36:26)*

> *For who has known the mind of the Lord, that he should instruct Him? But we have the mind of Christ. (1 Corinthians 2:16)*

A NEW SPIRIT

> *And be renewed in the spirit of your mind.. (Ephesians 4:23)*

> *And do not get drunk with wine, for that is dissipation, but be billed with the Spirit. (Ephesians 5:18)*

When one is born again in the spirit, we are joined together with the Lord by the Holy Spirit who is given to us.

> *But the one who joins himself to the Lord is one spirit with Him. (1 Corinthians 6:17)*

The Christian life and walk involves Christ living His life through us (Galatians 2:20) and daily walking in the spirit (Galatians 5:16).

A NEW MIND

> *For who has known the mind of the Lord, or who became His counselor? (Romans 11:34)*

> *And He who searches the hearts knows what the mind of the Spirit is, because He intercedes for the saints according tot he will of God. (Romans 8:27)*

Even though we have the mind of Christ, we should continue to be renewed in the mind of our spirit. The word renewed in Ephesians 4:23 does not mean to change as different, but to change as recent. The Spirit of the Lord does not change in character or nature, but we need to hear His voice for *the now*.

A NEW HEART

For the word of God is living and active and sharper than any two-edged sword, and piercing as far as the division of soul and spirit, of both joints and marrow, and able to judge the thought and intentions of the heart. (Hebrews 4:12)

Not by way of eye service, as men-pleasers, but as slaves of Christ, doing the will of God from the heart. (Ephesians 6:6)

In that they show the work of the Law written in their hearts, their conscience bearing witness, and their conscience bearing witness, and their thoughts alternately accusing or else depending them. (Romans 2:15)

⟨   The conscience of the Spirit

> *The spirit of man is the lamp of the Lord, searching all the innermost parts of his being. (Proverbs 20:27)*

⟨   The thoughts and intents "hidden springs of a person's life (Vine's)

A. REPOSITIONING RELATIONSHIPS

Involves a repositioning of relationships and refocusing of passion toward God and His Kingdom, then family, then relationship with others.

> *But seek first His Kingdom and His righteousness and all these things shall be added to you. (Matthew 6:33)*

B. REPOSITIONING MINISTRY

> *For through the grace given to me I say to every man among you not to think more highly of himself than he ought to think; but to think so as to have sound judgment, as God has allotted to each a measure of faith. For just as we have many members in one body and all the members do not have the same function, so we, who are many, are one body in Christ, and individually members one of another. And since we have gifts that differ according tot he grace given to us, let each exercise them accordingly: if prophecy, according to the proportion of his faith; service in his serving; or he who teaches, in his teaching; or he who exhorts, in his exhortation; he who gives, with liberality; he who leads, with diligence; he who shows mercy, with cheerfulness. (Romans 12:3-8)*

> *Hanani, one of my brothers, and some men from Judah came; and I asked them concerning the Jews who had escaped and had survived the captivity, and about Jerusalem. And they said to me, "The remnant there in the province who survived*

the captivity are in great distress and reproach, and the wall of Jerusalem is broken down and its gates are burned with fire." (Nehemiah 1:2-3)

Nehemiah 1-2

1. THE REPORT OF NEED

Ministry comes from a burden and a call. Usually the burden begins with either hearing about or seeing a need. Hearing or seeing a need does not necessarily constitute a call to meet the need, though it is a call to pray or to give. We should always pray about everything and never close our hearts to those in need.

2. WHEN THE NEED BECOMES A BURDEN

When the burden for a need can no longer be released through prayer and giving, it may be that God is calling us to help meet the need through some more personal contact.

3. THE CALL IS IN ACCORDANCE WITH HIS WORD

Ministry is to be in accordance with the Scriptures. The Word of the Lord came to our hearts personally.

4. RECEIVE COUNSEL FROM AUTHORITY

When our decisions affect the lives and investments of others, we should seek their authority and counsel. As we submit to proper authority, God will accomplish His will more effectively, more quickly or more safely. It is important to remember, however, that our ultimate authority should come from God.

Without consultation, plans are frustrated, but with many counselors they succeed. (Proverbs 15:21)

And when they had summoned them, they commanded them not to speak or teach at all in the name of Jesus. But Peter and John answered and said to them, "Whether it is right in the sight of God to give heed to you rather than to God, you be the judge; for we cannot stop speaking what we have seen and heard."(Acts 4:18-20)

5. **ALLOW FOR GOD'S TIMING**

6. **INVESTIGATE AND VALIDATE A NEED**

   Ministry is designed to meet need—Jesus Himself came to seek and save those who were lost. We must investigate whether the location, organization, church or opportunity is place where the ministry will fulfill our call or burden.

   > *"He who gives answer before he hears, it is folly and shame to him."*
   > *(Proverbs 18:13)*

7. **CONFIRM YOU MINISTRY WITH COWORKERS**

8. **CONTINUE WITH BOLDNESS AND CONFIDENCE IN GOD'S PURPOSES AND POWER**

C. OVERCOMING PASSIVITY

Passivity is the lack of courage, confidence and persistence to accomplish what God has called us to do.

D. CHARACTERISTICS OF PASSIVITY

1. **PROCRASTINATION:** Talking and thinking about plans and dreams, but not taking action

2. **DEPENDENCY:** Expecting others to take care of us and do for us what we should do for ourselves

3. **SHAME:** The faulty belief that "I am a mistake" instead of "I made a mistake"; A mistake can be corrected and a sin can be forgiven, but to believe you are a mistake causes you to feel less than redeemable.

4. **BLAMING:** Placing responsibility of others for our losses and failures

5. **DISCOURAGEMENT:** Becoming easily diverted from dreams and plans by discouragement and negative circumstances.

6. **INTIMIDATION:** Comparing ourselves with others and living with the fear that they can succeed but we cannot.

7. **CAUSES OF PASSIVITY**

8. **FEAR OF FAILURE**

9. **FEAR OF REJECTION**

10. **FEAR OF DEATH**

E. THE SPIRIT OF POWER

To understand the meaning of power, one has to consider not physical strength, but rather the ability to choose, to decide, and to take action. The spirit of power is not about brute force, but spiritual authority and the ability to take control of one's own life and destiny by giving control to the Lordship of Christ and walking in His power and authority.

When the Holy Spirit expresses His power over the spirit of timidity and passivity, the following three qualities will be present.

1. **CREATIVENESS**

2. **INITIATIVE**

3. **EFFECTIVENESS**

C. THE SPIRIT OF LOVE

Whoever confesses that Jesus is the Son of God, God abides in him, and he in God. And we have come to know and have believed the love which God has for us. God is love, and the one who abides in love abides in God, and God abides in him. By this, the love is perfected with us, that we may have confidence in the day of judgment; because as He is, so also are we in this world. There is no fear in love; but perfect love casts out fear, because fear involves punishment, and the one who fears is not perfected in love. We love, because He first loved us. (1 John 4:15-19)

1. **DEVELOP A DISCIPLINED MIND**

2. **LEARN TO READJUST**

3. KEEP LEARNING

Restoring the Soul

Therefore, putting aside all filthiness and all that remains of wickedness, in humility receive the word implanted, which is able to save your souls. (James 1:21)

Man's soul is not born again, but is being transformed and renewed into the image of Jesus Christ. This renewal involves taking off the old man (lifestyle) and putting on the new. The ministry of the early church was essential in this process.

And they were continually devoting themselves to the apostles' teaching and to fellowship, to the breaking of bread and to prayer. And everyone kept feeling a sense of awe; and many wonders and signs were taking place through the apostles. And all those who had believed were together, and had all things in common; and they began selling their property and possessions, and were sharing them with all, as anyone might have need. And day by day continuing with one mind in the temple, and breaking bread from house to house, they were taking their meals together with gladness and sincerity of heart, praising God, and having favor with all the people. And the Lord was adding to their number day by day those who were being saved. (Acts 2:42-47)

ROLE	PRESENT RESULTS	RESTORATION PROCESS
Teaching	Replacing false belief system with truth	**REFRAMING** Looking at life experiences with God's interpretation
Fellowship	Replacing wrong relationships with healthy relationships	**REBONDING** Giving God our whole heart and committing ourselves to those to whom He commits us
Breaking Bread	Replacing immature human response with God's wisdom	**REANCHORING** Experiencing new memories through experiences, rituals, etc.
Prayers	Replacing human standards and boundaries with God's standards	**REBUILDING** Giving reality to life situations

	with God's standards	
Mission	Replacing lack of purpose and joy with a new vision and enthusiasm	**REDIRECTING** Repositioning relationship and plans to fulfill God's plan

Authorized Site and Use License

Definitions

The "Licensed Property" is the *Christian Life School of Theology Global course contents and delivery systems*, hereafter referred to as "Curriculum." The "Owner" of the Curriculum is Christian Life School of Theology Global and is protected by United States and foreign copyright and other intellectual property laws. The "Authorized Site Licensee" is the party or representative of the party entering into this agreement with CLST Global. An "Authorized User" is any staff member of the Licensee, authorized representative, Locally Authorized Teacher, or student using any or all elements of the Licensed Property. The "Site" is the CLEN member school, its programs and students. The "Site" may also be an individual Distance Education student entering into this agreement.

Agreement

Christian Life School of Theology Global hereby grants to the designated Authorized Site Licensee, and the Licensee hereby accepts, a personal, non-exclusive, revocable, non-transferable License to access and use the Curriculum subject to the terms and conditions set forth herein. CLST Global grants to the Licensee and/or all Authorized Users a license to use the Curriculum at the Licensee's Site. All prior agreements, representations, and communications relating to the same subject are superseded by this Agreement. This Agreement may not be modified other than by a written document signed by an authorized representative of each party.

Terms

The Licensed Property may only be used for purposes of education or other non-commercial use. Content will not be used or shared outside of the Licensees' Site. This agreement does not permit anyone other than Authorized Users to use the Curriculum nor permit Authorized Users to use the Curriculum for any uses other than Authorized Uses. Licensee shall not use, or authorize or permit any Student or Staff to use, the Curriculum for any other purpose or in any other manner. The Licensee shall not use the Curriculum for commercial purposes, including but not limited to sale of the Curriculum or bulk reproduction or distribution of the Curriculum, or any portion thereof, in any form. The Licensee may not sell, lend, lease, rent, assign, or transfer the Curriculum to another party in any form. The Licensee may not translate, disassemble, or create derivative works based upon the Curriculum or any part thereof, without the written permission of CLST Global. The Licensee shall make reasonable efforts to prevent Unauthorized Uses of the Licensed Property.

Made in the USA
Middletown, DE
04 February 2022

60401824R00086